PUBLISHED *by* PARABLES
Earthly Stories with a Heavenly Meaning

I Still Have
A Praise In Me

Gail Marie Comminie

"The Lord is my strength and my defense; he has become my salvation. He is my God and I will praise him; my father's God and I will exalt him." -- Exodus 15:2

PUBLISHED *by* PARABLES
Earthly Stories with a Heavenly Meaning

I Still Have A Praise In Me
Gail Marie Comminie

Published By Parables
February, 2020

ISBN 978-1-951497-28-6
Printed in the United States of America

Readers should be aware that Internet Web sites offered as citations and/or sources for further information may have been changed or disappeared between the time this was written and the time it is read.

I Still Have

A Praise In Me

Gail Marie Comminie

"The Lord is my strength and my defense; he has become my salvation. He is my God and I will praise him; my father's God and I will exalt him." -- Exodus 15:2

PUBLISHED by PARABLES
Earthly Stories with a Heavenly Meaning

"In this life you have to go through the rain to see the rainbow"

"My times are in your hands", Psalm 31:19

Table Of Contents

Chapter 6
"Perilous Time"
2 Timothy 3:1-5, 'But mark this: There will be terrible times in the last days. People will be lovers of themselves, lovers of money, boastful, proud, abusive, disobedient to their parents, ungrateful, unholy, without love, unforgiving, slanderous, without self-control, brutal, not lovers of good, treacherous, rash, conceited, lovers of pleasure rather than lovers of God—having a form of godliness but denying its power. Having nothing to do with such people."

Chapter 7
"Stress of a Black Women"
Philippians 4:6-7, "Do not be anxious about anything, but in every situation, by prayer and petition, with thanksgiving, present your requests to God. And the peace of God, which transcends all understanding, will guard your hearts and your minds in Christ Jesus."

Chapter 8
"The Character of Love in The Home, by Pastor Vernon Alexander Sr.
1 Timothy 3:1-5, "Here is a trustworthy saying: Whoever aspires to be an overseer desires a noble task. Now the overseer is to be above reproach, faithful to his wife, temperate, self-controlled, respectable, hospitable, able to teach, not given to drunkenness, not violent, but gentle, not quarrelsome, not a lover of money. He must manage his own family well and see that his children obey him, and he must do so in a manner worthy of full respect. If anyone does not know how to manage his own family, how can he take care of God's Church?"
(Ten Commandments for The Home)
Psalm 28:9, "Save thy people and bless thine inheritance."

Chapter 9
"The Best Is Yet to Come" by Rev. Joseph Comminie Jr.
1 Corinthians 2:7-9, "No, we declare God's wisdom, a mystery that has been hidden and that God destined for our glory before time began. None of the rulers of this age understood it, for if they had, they would not have crucified the Lord of glory. However, as it is written: "What no eye has seen, what no ear has heard, and what no human mind has conceived" the things God has prepared for those who love Him."

Chapter 10:
"God to Return"
2 Timothy 4:8, "There is laid up for me a crown of righteousness, which the Lord, the righteous judge, shall give me at that day: and not to me only, but unto all them that love his appearing."
Psalm 27

Gail Marie Comminie

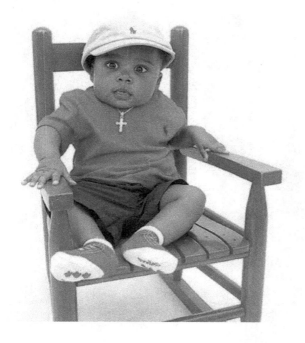

I am dedicating this book "I Still Have Praise In Me" to my
Grandson, Ja'Quan Joseph Comminie

Gail Comminie is a resident of Edgard, Louisiana and the daughter of the Late Jessel Sr and Late Eunice Smith. She is married to Rev. Joseph Comminie Jr. They have 4 children, Tammy Lynette Gullage, Shantel Comminie (Shannon Sr) Octave, Joseph "J.J." (Mtisa) Comminie III and Jamaal Anthony (Ranada) Comminie, 11 grandchildren (Anastasia, Leonard Jr. and Larenz Gullage, Shannon Jr. and Shayler Octave, Jeremiah Comminie, Jamaal Jr. and Ja'Quan Comminie, Syan and Randall Clark, Danasha Harris, 3 great grand-children (Aubrie Lynette Gullage, Jaceon and Jason DeBerrry.

Gail is an enthusiastic Christian, has been active in the Church most of her life and she loves writing.
Why This Book

On this life journey we will face many temptations, problems, illnesses and obstacles. God never promised us that this life will be easy or trouble free, but God did promise that He will never leave us or forsake us (Hebrews 13:5). He will always be there.

Why I Wrote This Book

This book is written to help and encourage others as they face life challenge.

One day, we the believers will all be with Jesus in Heaven. What a time that will be. We are going to the land of "NO MORE" (Revelation 21:4). The Best is Yet To Come so because of this, "I Still Have A Praise In Me!"
Recognition and Thanks:

Special Thanks

Thank You to my Husband of 47 years, Rev. Joseph Comminie Jr. who has encouraged me to write.

I love you more each passing day. The road has not always been easy, but we serve a God that is able!

Special thanks to my family, The Samuel, The Smith and The Comminie.

Thanks be to God the Father, who gave His Son to die for my sins.

Philippians 4:3, "I can do all things through Christ who strengthen me."

I Still Have A Praise In Me

Introduction

I have always considered myself to be a strong person. I have always believed that I was strong in the Word. When my Grandson was born, my faith was put to a test. My Grandson, Ja'"Quan Joseph, was born September 7, 2017, weighting 8lbs and 6 oz at Oak Bend Medical Center in Houston, Texas. He is the second son of my youngest son, Jamaal Sr. and Ranada Comminie. Ja'Quan has an older brother, Jamaal Anthony Comminie Jr. Right after his birth, he began having difficulty breathing and was not getting enough oxygen, He was airlifted to Houston Methodist Hospital ICU. He was diagnosed with HLHS (Hypoplastic Left Heart Syndrome) which is a birth defect that affects the normal blood flow through the heart. It is one type of congested heart defect. On September 11, 2017, just four days after his birth, he had open heart surgery and another open-heart surgery was performed when he was 5 months old. His next surgery is scheduled when he is 3-5 years old. Ja'Quan has been through a lot, but this little boy is strong. He has taught me a lot about the power of prayers. God is a Healer. Through it all I Still Have A Praise in Me.

In my life I've had to endure much. I've gone through sickness and am still facing illness. I've had to endure the loss of my parents, my brother, my niece, my brothers-in-law, aunts, friends and other close family and friends. I've had family problems. I've had problems in my marriage, finance, and other worries. I have learned to endure and to trust in God. I have learned to give it all to Him.

The Bible teaches that human suffering and problems are inescapable. We must accept it as an integral part of life. Job 14:1 said, "Man that is born of a woman is of few days, full of trouble. Our live has its beginning in suffering. Life's span is marked by

pain and tragedies and our lives end with the enemy called death. The person who expects to escape the pains of suffering and disappointments simply has no knowledge of the Bible, of history, or life.
The Bible teaches that suffering and pains is a part of life in a sinful world. Paul said, Roman 8:18, "For I reckon that the sufferings of this present time are not worthy to be compared with the glory which shall be revealed in us."

To everyone I say to look toward Heaven, look beyond the clouds and you will see that the suffering, pain and troubles that we are undergoing here are nothing compared to the glory that God has prepared for you in Heaven.

Why worry when you can Pray!

Many of us have earnest, persistent prayers that seem to go unanswered. But we can be assured that God does care, and he hears all our requests. He urges us to continue to walk closely with Him, being joyful in hope, patient in affliction, faithful on prayer. We can lean on Jesus.

Psalm 100:3-4, "Know that the Lord, He is God; it is He who made us, and not we ourselves; we are His people, and the sheep of His pasture. Enter into His gates with thanksgiving, and into His courts with praise; be thankful unto him and bless His name."

Chapter 1:

"It's All About Him"
John 3:16, "God so love the world that He gave His one and only
Son (Jesus Christ), that whosoever believes in Him shall not
perish, but have eternal life."

Colossians 1: 17, "He is before all things, and in Him all things
hold together."

Jesus is the Son of God, come down from heaven. He is the
serpent Moses wrote about in Numbers 21: 4-9. He is the Father's
Love Gift. He was lifted, and He died on a Cross for the sins of
the whole world. Everyone who look up to Him in faith will
receive eternal life. The Good News is that God sent His Son to
die for my and your sins! Jesus died in our place, so we could
have a relationship with God and be with Him forever.

Romans 5:8, "God demonstrate His own love towards us, in that
while we were yet sinners, Christ died for us."

But it didn't end with His death on the Cross. He rose again and
still lives. Jesus is the only way to God.

John 14:6, "I am the way, and the truth, and the life; no one comes
to the Father, but through Me."

We can't earn our salvation. We are saved by God's Grace when
we have faith in His Son, Jesus Christ. I first had to believe that I
was a sinner, Christ died for my sins and ask Him for forgiveness.
Then I had to turn from my sins (repentance). Jesus knows, and
Jesus loves me. I had to trust Him as Savior and follow Him as
Lord.

When we travel, we sometimes use a road map or GPS to get to our destination. Just one wrong turn can take us where we don't want to go or keep us from going where we want to go. We face and experience many roadblocks along the way. When we are lost on the road, we either check the map again or we stop and ask for direction.

Not all roads lead to God. There is a roadblock which keeps man from reaching God, no matter what road he takes. That roadblock is sin. But God has provided a map—THE BIBLE—and He has provided One who knows the way and can give direction—JESUS CHRIST. Christ said, "No Man comes to the Father but by me." Jesus gives us direction to Him, and He gives us daily directions of the Father's will for our lives. Like the directions on the road maps or direction from someone along the way as we travel, we can either follow them to get to our destinations or we can ignore them and get lost.

Just remember Jesus did not say, "I am one of the ways or one of the roads you can take to get to the Father." Jesus said, "I am The Way." So be determined to follow Christ and never be lost.

It is all about Him/Jesus! Romans 4:25, "He (Jesus) was delivered over to death for our sins and was raised to life for our justification."

Do we look at ourselves, our trials, our problems when we are suffering? Do we live under the circumstances instead of above the circumstances? Do we look at the One who knew more suffering than we are able to conceive? In Isaiah 53, the suffering of Christ is so vividly told that it sounds like it was eyewitness. But it was predicted by a man who wrote of Jesus suffering eight hundred years before the event.

Jesus came on a mission of love and mercy. He was sent by His Father. An Angel announced His conception and gave Him His Name. Matthew 1:21, "She (Mary) will give birth to a son, and

14

you are to give him the name Jesus, because He will save his people from their sins."

The birth of Jesus was different from every other birth, He was conceived by the Holy Spirit in Mary's womb and born with a sinless nature. He is "GOD with Us" and "He is also GOD like us." because He took our nature and entered human life and experiences. What a wonderful Savior!

The Son of the Eternal Father became human. He assumed our human nature with all its infirmities, weakness and capacity for suffering. He left all of Heaven Glory and became a child of the poorest parents. He became a servant and to minister rather than to be minister to.

As creatures created by God, we submit to the Creator who made us. We are the sheep who submit to the Shepherd who died for us. We are blessed and we are privileged to offer spiritual sacrifices to the Lord. We offer songs of praise, good works and material gifts. Because of who Jesus is and what He does for us, He is certainly worthy of our joyful thanks. Because of who we are, we will love our brothers and sisters. We will help strangers. We will strive to live above lust and covetousness, and we will not be led astray by false doctrines.

At Calvary our sins were put on Christ's account. When we trust Christ, God puts Christ's righteousness on our account. 2 Corinthians 5:21, "For He made Him who knew no sin to be sin for us, that we might become the righteousness of God in Him."

What can be more blessed than to know that our sins are forgiven? Because Jesus is my Savior and all those who believe and trust in His finished work. He saves me and you from the penalty of sin. Because He is our Lord, by His Holy Spirit, gives me and you power over sin as we walk daily with Him, far from the presence of sin.

Hebrew 9:28, "So Christ was offered once to bear the sins of many. To those who eagerly wait for Him, He will appear a second time, apart from sin, for salvation."

The Blood that purchased eternal redemption came not from unwilling animals, but from the Son of God who willing laid down His life for you (John 10: 14-28). The spotless Lamb of God had to die only once. The sacrifice need not be repeated.

Only because Jesus is God and we have confessed Him as Savior and Lord, can He bestow, and we receive these benefits…this blessed assurance and hope. Romans 10:9, "that if you confess with your mouth the Lord."

God is Love. 1 John 4:8-9, "He who does not love does not know God; for God is love. In this the love of God was made manifest among us. That God sent his only Son into the world, so that we might live through him."

From Genesis to Revelations, from earth's greatest tragedy to earth's greatest triumph, the dramatic story of man's lowest depths and God's highest heights can be summed up in twenty-five beautiful words: "For God so loved the world, that He gave His only begotten Son, that whosoever believeth in Him should not perish, but have everlasting life." John 3:16

Many people misunderstand the attribute of God's nature which is love. "God is Love" does not means that everything is sweet, beautiful and happy and that God's Love could not possibly allow punishment for sin.

God's holiness demands that all sin be punished, but God's Love provided a plan of redemption and salvation for sinful man. God's Love provided the Cross of Jesus Christ by which man can have forgiveness and cleansing. It was the love of God that sent Jesus Christ to that Cross.

Who can describe or measure the love of God? The Bible is a
revelation of the fact that God is love. When we preach justice, it
is justice tempered with love. When we preach righteousness, it is
righteousness founded on love. When we preach atonement, it is
atonement planned by love. Provided by love, given by love,
finished by love, necessitated because of love. When we preach
the resurrection of Christ, we are preaching the miracle of love.
When we preach the return of Christ, we are preaching the
fulfillment of love. Billy Graham Daily Devotion, November 3,
2018

A little more than thirty years after His birth, Jesus asked His
disciples, "Who do people say the Son of Man is?" (Matthew
16:13). They give the responses others had given: John the
Baptist, Elijah, maybe another prophet. Then Jesus made it
personal: "Who do you say I am? (v.15). Peter replied, "You are
the Messiah, the Son of the living God" (v 16).

At Christmas, many celebrate without a thought about who the
baby really is. Is Christmas just a heartwarming story about a baby
born in a stable? Or did our Creator visit His Creation and become
one of us? At Christmas time, lavish or small, we as believers
should honor the Messiah who came to redeem His Creation. Who
do you say Jesus is?

Do you know Him? I mean do you really know who He is?
Judas was one who beheld Him. Judas one of the original
disciples, but never knew Him. Judas betrayed Jesus with a kiss.
Instead of asking for forgiveness, he committed suicide. Don't be
like Judas? Don't just know of Him, know Him as your personal
Lord and Savior.

It is not about me; it is not about you; it's about Him.
No love is more beautiful than the love of God. Psalm 136:6, "his
love endures forever." Love is the master key that opens the gates
of happiness. If God so love us, we ought to love each other.
Love is the message of the Cross, the Cross is the power of God.

John 14:6, "he is the way, the truth and the life." Philippians 4:3, "I can do all things through Christ who strengthen me".
Life is not measure by the breath we take, but the moment that takes our breath away. So, we by faith lift up our eyes to God. Continue to live and love each other and each day as a gift. Where there is faith, there is love. Where there is love, there is peace. Where there is peace, there is God. Where God is, nothing is missing.

Human knowledge and technology reach only so far. You and I can never evade God's awareness throughout every moment of our lives. David prayed, "Where can I go from your Spirit? Where can I flee from your presence? If I go up to the heavens, you are there; If I make my bed in the depths, you are there" Psalm 139:7-8. "Such knowledge is too wonderful for me," he exclaims gratefully (v6).

God chooses to know us because He loves us. He cares enough not only to observe our lives but also to enter into them and make them new. He drew near through Jesus's life, death and resurrection, so we can know Him in return and love Him for eternity. We can never go beyond the reach of God's Love. How does the thought that God knows and love us completely encourage us? How will we reach out to others with His love today? Thank you for always seeing me, God! Help me to live each day with a growing awareness of Your presence and perfect Love.

We don't have to guess what God is like, and we don't have to stare in the sky and wonder, is God up there? God has already let us see who He is by sending His Son Jesus to earth, the Father made Himself known to us. Jesus was God "appeared in the flesh" (1Timothy 3:16). Anyone who has seen me has seen the Father" (John 14:9).

This is the good news of Christmas—that God has shown us what He is like in the person of His Son. He left Heaven's glory and came down to earth to be born of a virgin. All strength, character and power of the infinite God was found in the baby that Mary cradled in a Bethlehem manger. He was the "image of the visible God, the firstborn over all creation" (Colossians 1:15). And "in Him all things were created.... all things hold together" (v 16-17). When we celebrate Jesus's birth, remember who He is. In Him we see the holiness, the grace and the Love of the eternal God. At Christmas, GOD DID STEP OUT OF HEAVEN!!!!

The manger was the first step in God's Journey to Calvary's Cross! The question for us is this" is our Christmas still only a story about a baby or is it more, a story about a Person into whom the baby grew, who can redeem the world from its sins and who call us into partnership with His great and mighty purposes? Jesus came at Christmas to show us the "fullness of God (Colossians 1:19). He came to "reconcile to himself all things…by making peace through the blood" (v.20). It is only as we see the birth of Jesus in light of His crucifixion and resurrection that we are able to grasp the full meaning of His coming. We should Thank God for the gift of His Son. The baby grew up and died for all our sins. Christ the savior is Born!

His love endures forever.

I Thank You God, I am Still Alive and I Still Have a Praise In Me!

Chapter 2

"So, You Think You've Got It All"
2 Peter 1:3, "as His divine power has given to us all that pertain to life and godliness, through the knowledge of Him who called us by glory and virtue."

What is it that I need from the Lord? What is it that I need the Lord to do for me? Do I need more money or wealth? Do I need health? Do I need fame? Do I need a big house or an expensive car? What is it I need from God? I've got it all! That is how some people may feel. It all about them. So, they think!

Many Christians believe that God can do anything but at the same time believe, they don't have enough. We are begging God for a healing, begging God for a car, money, bigger houses, we are begging God. The truth is we've already got it.

The Bible says, we've already got it.

Healing, finance, joy, peace, long suffering and everything we need have been provided. Galatians 5:22-23, "But the fruit of the Spirit is, love, joy, peace, longsuffering, kindness, goodness, faithfulness, gentleness, self-control. Against there is no law."

Everything I need, everything you need is there in me because I am born again. It is in my spirit, in your spirit. God has already poured out His love toward me. Roman 5:5b. "the love of God has been poured out in our hearts by the Holy Spirit who has given to us." God loves me and you whether we feel it or not. God's love has been poured out in our hearts, in our Spirit. God has already provided everything we need.

If you are sick and need a healing, 1 Peter 2:24, "who Himself bore our sins in His own body on the tree, that we, having died to sins, might live for righteousness—by whose stripes you were healed." I have the same power in me that raised Jesus from the dead living in me. Ephesians 1:19-20, "and what is the exceeding greatness of His power toward us who believes, according to the working of His mighty power, which He worked in Christ when He raised Him from the dead and seated Him at His right hand in the heavenly places."

When we get the doctors' reports or feel pain, we are quick to ask, "I am sick Lord, will you please heal me? You already have the victory. Don't just move toward it, come from it. Jesus has already provided everything we need. We are blessed with all spiritual blessings.

When Jesus died on the cross, He said, "It Is Finished", John 19:30. Ephesians 1:20 tells us that he is seated at the Father's right hand. He is not working anymore. He had already done it. It Is Finished!

Do you need to be healed? It's already done. Jesus bored our stripes in His body over 2000 years ago. Do you need to be saved? 1 John 2:2, 'he is the propitiation for our sins: and not for ours only, but also for the sins of the whole world." God has provided a way for the whole world to be forgiven. Put your faith in Jesus.

God has already commanded His blessing on our finances. He has already given us love, joy and peace. So many of us are missing it. We know that God can do anything and all things, but we don't think that God has done enough. We are in a position of unbelief. If you want a healing, the proper way is found in Proverb 18:21, "Death and life are in the power of the tongue."

You can release the power over sickness and disease. Speak an end to the sickness and command it to leave, say, "God, I speak the life that you've already put on the inside of me."

We as Believers, as Christians, need to begin to believe that things happened that we cannot see, taste, smell, hear or feel. For instance, we know that our televisions, cell phones, radios all work by signals. We can't see it, but we trust it to work and provide the signals we need. We need to apply this concept to our Spiritual Life. Don't limit God. God has all power and His signal; His power never fails or go out. God has everything we need.

Have you ever searched something only to you find out it did not bring the satisfaction you thought it would? All you got was just a whole lot of frustrations and disappointments. We are looking for fulfillment in the things of this world that will never ever completely satisfy us or fulfill. We will always want more. We look for love, acceptance and joy in our careers, in money, in power and in all sort of material things. If these things really brought us any kind of lasting fulfillment or joy, someone would have written a book on it. "I Found Joy, Love and Fulfillment in Material Things". Put Jesus first in your life and turn your life around. By putting Jesus Christ first, everything else would fall into place. You will discover where the love, joy, peace and acceptance you've been searching for is to be found.

We should never assume we know it all. Trust God from the bottom of your heart. Don't ever try to figure out everything on your own. Stop and listen for God's voice in everything you do and everywhere you go. God is the one who will keep you on track. Don't assume you know it all. Run to God! Run from evil! Honor God in everything you do. Honor God with everything you own. Always give God the first and the best.

Remember we make plans, but God always has the last word. We may even think that everything we do is right or good, but the Lord judges our motives and our thoughts. Always ask God to bless your plans before carrying it. We make plans, but God directs our actions.

Remember to always pay attention to what you are taught and trust the Lord and He will continue to direct your path.

So, you might think you have it all…correction. GOD got it and He has provided for you and me. There is nothing for us to worry about. What are you worried about? Why? No matter what, "I Still Have a Praise In Me."

Chapter 3

"When Trials Begins"
Hebrew 12:2, "Looking unto Jesus, the author and finisher of our faith, who for the joy that was set before Him endured the cross, despising the shame, and has set down at the right hand of the throne of God."

Where did we ever get the idea that the Christian life is to be a careful life without trials? When trials come, we sometimes act as if God is out of town or on vacation. We question God: Why is this happening to me? What did I do to deserve this? I did when I first had my stroke. After all, I attend Church regularly. I am a Sunday School Teacher. I am on the Deaconess Board. I tithe and give my offering. I have witnessed for you, and I am a Minister's Wife. So why God am I going through this? Why did this happen to me? Have you ever felt that way? I am sure I am not alone.

In the Scripture, you will see that Jesus said, "in this world you shall have trials and tribulations." Jesus didn't say that I could have tribulation or that if you aren't a good person, tribulation will come your way. Jesus stated that you will have tribulation. This is as certain as growing old.

Jesus also said that if He was persecuted, I would be persecuted too, because "no servant is greater than his master." When someone is persecuting you for your belief, they are persecuting the Christ in you. Jesus said, be of good cheer, I have overcome the world." Jesus is saying that while they are persecuting you (or persecuting the Jesus in you) don't worry about it. Jesus has already overcome the world, which is the source of your trials and tribulations.

Just imagine that you were worried about a financial debt and someone told you, don't worry, I will pay. What a relief! Imagine the load off your mind, the experience of relief you felt. This is what Jesus wants us to experience and the attitude to have in the midst of our trials, God wants us to look to Jesus, the Author and Finisher of our Faith. Jesus has already overcome similar trials and tribulations and will give us the same power to do the same. Jesus is waiting for us to ask.

Look at Job. Job did not know that Satan had gotten permission from God before he could touch Job, much less Job's possessions. When Job lost everything, he did not say, "The Lord gave, and the devil has taken away," but, "The Lord gave, and The Lord has taken away'; may the name of the Lord be praised", Job 1:21.

So, whenever we are hurt it is important to remember that God Himself has allowed it for a purpose. God does not take away our trials or carry us over them, but strengthens us through them. Nowhere in the Bible does it teaches that Christians are to be exempt from tribulations. It does teach that the Christian can face tribulations, crisis, calamity, personal suffering with a supernatural power not available to the person outside of Christ. Many Christians have learned the secret of contentment and joy in trials. I have seen and met some happy Christian who have trials and misfortunes. Some have life-long illnesses, but they still give God the Praise. They have every reason to complain, being denied so many privileges and pleasures that they see others enjoy and do things they use to do. Yet they still praise God. They have learned to give thanks always and for everything in the Name of our Lord Jesus Christ to God the Father, Ephesians 5:20.

As Christians we can rejoice in tribulation, in trials because we have eternity in view. When the pressure is on, just look beyond the present predicament to the glories of Heaven. The thought of the future, life with Jesus, makes trials of the present seem light and transient. Don't forget what Christ Himself have gone through

26

for our Salvation and for us to suffer for His name's sake is a gift rather than a cross.

In the Bible, we read where the disciples were on a boat and Jesus was on the boat. Matthew 8:23-27 Jesus was asleep in the bottom of the boat. The sky became dark, the wind begins to blow, the rain came. Where was Jesus? The disciples went to Jesus and when they found Him, they said, Lord, save us! We're going to drown!" Jesus replied, you of little faith, why are you so afraid?" Then Jesus got up and rebuked the winds and the waves, and it was completely calm. He said, "Peace" and they were still. The wind stopped, and the sea was calm. Jesus then turn to the disciples and rebuked them with a question, "Where is your faith?" In verse 27, the disciples were amazed and asked, "what kind of man is this? Even the winds and the waves obey him!" These disciples had seen Jesus do many things, heal many people, done many miracles. So why were they worried? The disciples forgot that this was Jesus on board. During this frightening time in their life when everything looks like it was lost, Jesus was on board and He is still on board.

During the difficult times in our lives. Don't forget that Jesus is in the boat with us. No matter how the wind blows, or the rain falls, or the storms come, Jesus is there with us. He is on board. He will bring peace to the storm. Put your trust and faith in Him. Isaiah 43:2, "And surely I am with you always, to the very end of the age."

What a joy and comfort to know that Jesus is with us in the boat, even when it looks like He is asleep. He has all power in heaven and on earth. He is everywhere.

We have the power to triumph over tragedy, even in situations which might seem hopeless and unredeemable to the world. The key to understanding tragedy is to understand its source. Death, pain and tragedy came into the world because of sin. Many people blame God for tragedy, but James tells us that "every good and perfect gift comes from the Father of lights." Tragedy is a result of sin having entered the world. But Christ triumphed over tragedy and He wants us to do the same, and in such triumph, God is glorified. Triumphing over tragedy is a form of witnessing for Christ. When something tragic happens to us such as the loss of a loved one or the loss of a job, the unbelievers are watching us to see if we react differently than they would. If there is no difference, if we despair as unbelievers might, how is God honored? How do we testify of Christ and His Power?

Remember, 2 Corinthians 2:14, says, "Now thanks be unto God, which always causes us to triumph in Christ."

Philippians 4:13, For I can do everything God asks me to with the help of Christ who gives me the strength and power."

If I get born again, will all my problems go away? No, but you will have the power to deal with them. Think about that. Our problems won't go away, but we will have the power to deal with them. The power to deal with problems produces a muscular Christian who can do combat with the evil one. If we could dismiss all our problems with a single stroke, we would be the shallowest of individuals. We would be spiritual "wimps" unable to fight our way out of a paper bag!

The prayer of Jesus in the Garden of Gethsemane is perhaps the greatest prayer ever said. Our Lord asked that His cup of crucifixion, which was about to be thrust upon Him, might be taken away. But then, He said, "Nevertheless not as I will, but as thou wilt," Matthew 26:39. What a Prayer! What Strength! What Power!

When the Apostle Paul asked God to remove his "thorn in the flesh," God did not remove it, saying instead, "My grace is sufficient for thee," 2 Corinthians 12:9. Christ desires to be with you in whatever crisis you may find yourself. Call upon His Name. See if He will not do as He promised He would. He will not make your problems go away, but He will give you the power to deal with and overcome them.

When we find ourselves flattened on the cold ice of life's hardship, is there a healing hand nearby? If so, it might be from God. Or when someone needs a friend, could we be God's answer to life them up? If it appears that no one is nearby to lift us to our feet, we can find comfort in knowing that God is our ever-present help (Psalm 46:1). As we reach out to Him, He's ready to steady us with a His firm grip. He is there to help me when life knocks me down. Thank you, God, for the people you've use to encourage and strengthen me. God, you are the most faithful friend I have.

When things happen, when trials come, when you see no way out, just remember you will be, and you are alright. God's got you. You just have to go through the storms. "God, How Great Thou Art!!
Life is not measure by the breath we take, but the moment that take our breath away. So, we by faith, lift our eyes to God.

I was at the crossroad in my life. I was at my breaking point. I did not know which way to turn or what to do. I couldn't go left, I couldn't go right, and I was not going back. What was I to do? It was when I remember who I am, I am a Child of the Most High God! At the lowest time in my life, God was there and still is there. Whenever you think that things can't get any worst, God is there. When families and friends turn their back on you, God is there. When sickness comes, when death comes, God is there. When finance is low or gone, God is still there. Acknowledge Him as your Lord and Savior.

Lord help me to remember that nothing is to happen to me today that you and I can't get through together.
Life storms come in many forms, hurricanes, earthquakes, floods, unexpected problems in marriage or with children, the loss of a loved one, or the sudden loss of finances. So much we value can be swept away in a moment.

Amid the storms, Scripture points us to the safest place, "God is our refuge and strength, an ever-present help in trouble. Therefore, we will not fear, though the earth give way" Psalm 46:1-2. Troubles come, but God outlasts them all. Those who run to the Savior discover that He can't be shaken. In the arms of His eternal love, we will find peace. Amid life's unpredictable storms, how does God give you peace? How do you intend to run to Him today? God the one who is greater than the storm, help me to place every fear in Your hands today and rest in your unfailing Love.

Whatever troubles overtakes us, whatever evils, Jesus—The Lion of Judah—is with us (Revelation 5:5). No matter how alone we feel, our Savior is with us. No matter what fears ravage us, our God assures us that He is by our side. What is your greatest fear right now? How does God's promise to be with you encourage you?

"I Still Have A Praise In Me." Try God.

Chapter 4

"Surrender Self"
Mark 8 34-35, "Jesus said: Whoever will come after me, let him deny himself, and take up the cross and follow me, for whoever will save his life shall lose it; but whoever shall lose his life for my sake, and the gospel shall save it."

What is the secret of magic of a victorious Christian living? There is no magic formula. If any word could describe it, it would be "surrender". How do I surrender? The same way salvation comes to a sinner. There needs to be a confession of sin and a complete yielding of every area of life, personality and will to Jesus and you must have faith that Jesus will accept that commitment. It is not enough for us to have been confirmed or to have made a decision for Christ at the altar. We need to turn and renew our vows and covenant with the Lord. We need to take an inventory and have a spiritual checkup. Christ is calling Christians to cleansing, to dedication, to consecration, to full surrender. Our response will make the difference between success and failure in our spiritual life. It will make the difference between needing help and being able to help others.

When we surrender, it will revolutionize our habits, our prayer life, our Bible Reading, our giving, our testimony and our Church relationship. This is the Christian hour of decision! For the Believer, The Christian who has been suffering defeat or have been outside the will of God or do not know the power, the thrill and joy that Christ can bring, I beg you to surrender every area of your life. Please give yourself wholly to Christ.

You try it your way and it didn't work. Try God!

Romans 12: 1-2, "I beseech you therefore brethren, by the mercies of God, which is your reasonable service. And do not be conformed to this world, but be transformed by the renewing of your mind, that you may prove what is that good and acceptable and perfect will of God."

Transformed means to be changed. We need a change, a spiritual change, a moral change. God is calling on all of us to make a surrender to His Son Jesus Christ. If we want to have forgiveness, peace and joy in our lives, then we must surrender to Him. We have to make a total surrender. He has to be Lord and He has to be the ruler in our lives. We have to trust God and allow Him to be in total control. We put it all in His hands.

Have you ever taken a flight on an airplane? What thoughts goes through your mind? If you are like me, I am sure you have some fear. What if the plane crashes? What kind of weather is ahead? All kinds of thoughts of what could go wrong is going through your head, but you still are determined to get on board. You get to the airport on time, you check in and then you take a seat and wait for your time to get on board. You get on board, take your seat, get instructions from the flight attendants and then you sit back and surrender to the plane and the pilot. You can't do anything about it, but trust the pilot knows how to fly the plane. You put your faith in the pilot, why not God? After all God is in control of the plane and the pilot. My faith is in God and I trust God to provide a safe trip for me and everyone on board. I surrender to Him.

The same when we face surgery. My faith is in God. I trust God to guide the knives and that the doctors are going to do the right thing. We have to surrender to God totally and completely. We can't hold anything back. We have surrendered our minds. Not only what we think, but how we think. We are careful what we put into our minds and the minds of our children. We are constantly repeating what we learn, and we reinforced it in our minds. What we remember influences us now and in the future.

Proverbs 23:7, "For as (a person thinks) in his hearts, so is he."

What do you think in your heart? What are you really like inside? There are two forces at work inside of you, one is satanic, and one is God. Don't let the devil corrupt your mind. Our children's behavior is being influences by what they see and hear. Have you seen some of the television commercials, the shows and movies? Have you listened to the music they listen to? It is all about violence. No wonder we have so many school shootings. No wonder we so many mass killings and destruction. Our minds and our children's minds are being saturated with violence, sex and whatever.

Philippians 2:5, "let this mind be in you which was also in Christ Jesus."

We have to surrender our body. The Bible says if you are Christian, your body does not belong to you. It belongs to God. The Bible says, our body is God's Temple, and He dwells in you if you really know Christ. Read Corinthians 3:16.

What does the Bible say about sex? If it weren't for sex, you and I would not be here. God created sex. He made us sexual human beings, men and women. Sex is being used for reasons for which God never intended. God intended that sex is to be within marriage, a man and a woman. Now we see the world fighting for their rights to do wrong. If you have made a mistake in this area, ask God to forgive you and change you and give you the power to resist temptation.

The Bible says, 1 Corinthians 6:9,10, "do not be deceived; Neither the sexually immoral nor idolaters nor adulterous will inherit the kingdom of God." To get to Heaven, we have to change.

Everybody is tempted. The devil tempts everybody, I have been tempted and so have you. Temptation is not a sin. It is when we yield to temptation that it becomes sin. We have to surrender to

Christ. Let Christ dominate your life and become Lord of your life. Let Him In. He is at the door knocking, open and invite Him in.

The word 'surrender' is defined as: to yield, give up or over, submit. In order to surrender your heart, body and soul to God, one must be willing to yield to the sovereign claim of a righteous God. We need to understand that man is separated from a Holy God by sin and there must be reconciliation. God has made provision for man to be reconciled to Himself and that provision is found in the once-for-all sacrifice made by the Lord Jesus Christ on the Cross.

Surrender. Let Go and Let God. He knows what's best. Stop striving and start abiding, Learning to let go of control is to stop striving. We don't have to strive to make our life turn out a certain way, we just have to abide in Him (John 15).

We have to confess and surrender our need for control. Some of us like being in control. It makes us feel like we have a purpose. Being a control freak isn't going to get you anywhere. Remember God holds it all together, so surrender your need to always be in control. Learn to trust. We have to let go of trying to figure out the how and why in life and trust that God understands more than we ever could. We have to be still and know that He is God. He is in control. Look at the parting of the Red Sea in Exodus 14. Moses tells the people, "Do not be afraid. Stand firm, the Lord will fight for you; you need only to be still." And you know what God did? He rescued them! He was in control the whole time, even when the enemy was on its way, ready to take the Israelites down. He can do the same for us when we trust and rest in Him. Always seek God. God holds the world in His Hand. We will never fully understand the power and extent of those hands if we're not tuned into and focused on Him. When we surrender control, wait and trust in God's plan, know that God will be faithful to lead us where He wants us to go. Seek God and He will direct your path.

34

A persistent worry or even a sinful thought that disrupts a prayer may become the centerpieces of our discussion with God. God wants us to be real as we talk with Him and open up about our deepest concerns, fears and struggles. He is not surprised by anything we mention. His interest in us is like the attention we would receive from close friends. That's why we're encouraged to give all our worries and cares to God, because he cares for us. Distractions don't have to derail our prayer.

Jesus says, "Whoever wants to be my disciple must dent themselves and take up their cross daily and follow me" (Luke 9:23). His path was one of self-denial and suffering, which can be hard to follow. But to be His effective disciples, we too are invited to put aside selfish desires and pick up spiritual burdens daily— serving others first instead of ourselves, for example—as we closely follow Him. When we walk close with God, follow His lead, and staying close to Him, we can appear as one. Then others won't see us, they'll see Him. "Wow!" Our lives are a window through which others can see Jesus.

We may experience pain that feels endless, situations that appears hopeless or waiting that seems unbearable. We may endure moments when the odds against us are stacked high and wide. We may not experience the healing we long for as we continue trusting Christ. But even then, Jesus invites us to keep reaching for Him and never give up hope and to believe He is always able, always trustworthy and always within reach. Have you recently surrendered in Jesus and trusted Him despite that challenge you faced? What hope have you found in in Him?
Jesus, thank You for reminding us that we're never out of Your reach or without Hope. You are able to do what no one else can do.
Christian service is working in the name of Jesus, not expecting to receive anything in return. This does not means working eight hours daily. It means helping others in need and working in the church and community. Christian service is giving and not looking

for anything in return. Christian service is doing and being; without looking for honor and recognition.

I, me, mine and myself can never be a part of serving and being a servant.

Question: Why can't the words I, me, mine and myself ever be a part of raising the standard of service?

Keep in your mind and know that a servant is not a getter, but a giver. A servant is not one who holds grudges, but a forgiver. A servant is not one who keeps score, but a forgetter. A servant is not a superstar, but a SERVANT!
Loves never fades or fails, John 3:16. God doesn't expect us to understand everything about Him, but to be willing and obedient servants, faithful to what is true and right. Circumstances may change, but God remains constant and does not break His promise. No matter what position in life we attain, we are always ripe for a downfall and must never let our guard down against sin and temptation. Read 1 Kings 9.

What is it I need to surrender to Jesus? What is it that you need to surrender to Jesus? We need to surrender all our doubts and fears, for they are our enemies to raising a Christian standard. We must surrender everything and everyone in our lives that separate us from the Love of God and raising the standard of God. We must surrender to Jesus by becoming clay in His hands so that He can mold us and make us into the vessel He chooses.

HYMN: "I SURRENDER ALL"

Thank You, God, for carrying me and my needs close to Your Heart. I surrender my life and these I love in Your care.

No matter what comes in your life, surrender to God and let God takes the lead. Through it all, "I Still Have a Praise In Me."

Chapter 5

"The Importance of A Prayer Life"
Romans 8:26, "In the same way, the Spirit helps us in our weakness. We do not know what we ought to pray for, but the Spirit himself intercedes for us through wordless groans."

How much do you pray? If someone were to examine my or your prayer life, would they find that you or I are more excited about watching our favorite TV program, visiting a friend, shopping or going to a function than talking to God? What kind of prayer life do I have? Do I pray only when I need something from God? Do I pray only when I am sick? Do I pray only when I am in trouble? Do I pray only when I am grieving or burden? Do I put God in my closet in a box and only take out when I need Him? When do I pray?

God's purpose is to make His children like His Son, and He will succeed. The Spirit intercedes for us and guides us as we pray and the circumstances of life work for our good, no matter how painful that may be.

Jesus considered prayer more important than food, for the Bible says that hours before breakfast, "very early in the morning, while it was still dark, Jesus got up, left the house and went off to a solitary place, where he prayed, Mark 1:35.

To the Son of God, prayer was more important than assembling and healing of great throngs. The Bible says, Luke 5:15-16, "Crowds of people came to hear Him and to be healed of their sickness. But Jesus often withdrew to lonely places and prayed."

The precious hours of fellowship with His Heavenly Father meant much more to our Savior than sleep, for the Bible says, Luke 6:12, Jesus went out into the hills to pray and spent the night praying to God."

He prayed at funerals and the dead were raised. He prayed over the five loaves and two fishes, and He fed a multitude with a little boy's lunch. While on the Cross He prayed, Luke 22:42, "Not my will, but yours."

And a way was made whereby sinful man might approach a Holy God. Prayer is not a futile cry of desperation born of fear and frustration. Many people pray only when they are under great stress, or in danger, or facing some crisis. There seems to be an instinct in man to pray in times of danger. If a Christian spent as much time praying as they do grumbling, they would soon find that they have nothing to grumble about.

1 Thessalonians 5:17, 23, "Pray without ceasing...and the very God of peace sanctify you wholly."

Remember that you can pray anytime and anywhere. We can pray while washing dishes, on our jobs, shopping, on the football field, driving our cars, getting our hair done, in school, in prison. You can pray and know that God hears. Prayer combined with Bible Study makes for a healthy life. The Bible says, "Pray without ceasing." If you have special prayers periods that you set aside during the day, your unconscious life will be saturated with prayer between that period. It is not enough for you to get out of bed in the morning and just bow your knee and repeat a few words or sentences. There should be periods in which you slip apart with God. For the overworked mother or father or someone living under extremely busy circumstances, this may be impossible. But here is where "prayer without ceasing" comes in. We pray as we work. As I said, we pray everywhere and any time.

The devil will fight you every step of the way. He will cause the baby to cry, the telephone to ring, someone to knock at the door. There will be many interruptions but keep at it. Don't be discouraged. Soon you will find that these periods of prayers are the greatest delight in your life. You will look forward to them with more anticipation than to anything else. Without constant, daily, systematic prayer, your life will seem barren, discouraging, and fruitless. Without constant prayer you never can know the inner peace that God wants to give you.

James 5:16, "Therefore confess your sins to each other and pray for each other so that you may be healed. The prayer of a righteous person is powerful and effective."

From one end of the Bible to the other, there is the record of those whose prayers have been answered, men who turned the tide of history by prayer; men who fervently prayed and God answered. Hezekiah prayed when the city was threatened by the invading army of the Assyrians under the leadership of Sennacherib and the entire army of Sennacherib was destroyed and the nation was spared another generation because the king prayed (2 Chronicles 32).

The problems of the world will never be settled unless our national leaders go to God in prayers, if only they would discover the power and wisdom that there is in reliance upon God. We could soon see the solution to the grave problems that face the world.

How wonderful it would be if the president, vice president, the senates and our elected leaders and officials, at the beginning of each sessions, to get on their knees before God! What a tremendous change there would be in all the affairs of government.

Elijah prayed, and God sent fire from heaven to consume the offering on the altars he had built in the presence of God's enemies.

Elisa prayed and the son of the Shunammite woman was raised from the dead.

Daniel prayed, and the secret of God was made known to him for the saving of his and his companions' lives and the changing of the course of history.

Paul prayed and hundreds of churches were born in Asia Minor and Europe. Peter prayed, and Dorcas was raised to life to have added years of service for Jesus Christ.

Make room for God in your life and in your heart. No room for Jesus? No room for the King of Kings? No, but room for others and for other things. There was no room for Jesus in the world that He had made—imagine!

Things have not really changed since that Bethlehem night two thousand years ago. God is still on the fringes of most of our lives. We fit Him in when it is convenient for us, but we become irritated when He makes demands on us. If God would only stay in His little box and come out when we pull the string.

Acts 6:4, (The Disciples said:) We will devote ourselves to prayer, and the ministry of the word.

We are to pray in times of adversity, lest we become faithless and unbelieving. We are to pray in times of prosperity, lest we become boastful and proud. We are to pray in times of danger, lest we become fearful and doubting. We need to pray in times of security, lest we become self-sufficient. Sinners, pray to a merciful God for forgiveness. Christian, pray for an outpouring of God's Spirit upon a willful evil, unrepentant world. Parents, pray that God may crown your home with grace and mercy. Children, pray for the salvation of your parents.

Satan trembles when he sees the weakest Saint upon his knees, so pray, Christian pray!

The model prayer which Jesus has given us concludes with, "Thine is the kingdom, and the power, and the glory." If we are to have our prayers answered, we must give God the glory. What a privilege is ours: the privilege of PRAYER! James 5:16, "The prayer of a righteous person is powerful and effective."

Many of us have earnest, persistent prayers that seem to go unanswered. But we can be assured that God does care, and He does hear all our requests. He urges us to continue to walk closely with Him, being "joyful in hope, patient in affliction, faithful in prayer", Roman 12:12. We can lean on Him. Let us draw closer to God with a sincere heart and with the full assurance that faith brings. Be persistent in prayer!

Our lives are so full. There is so much to be done. Are we in danger in all our busy activities of excluding from our hearts and the lives the One who made us? Do we have time enough to begin each day by reading God's Word and praying to the One who made us? Do we have time to make room for God in our prayers? Do we have time to ask God what He wants us to do?

A lot of young people have problems. Often crisis comes up and they have no one whom they feel they can share their problems. They can turn to the streets for answers, and often time are given wrong advice.

We have to pray that legislators will counteract the present law prohibiting prayer in schools and return prayer in school. Pray that our children will not have a desire to carry weapons in schools. Pray that the drug dealers will get saved and no longer be a part of the plan of Satan to use our children for drug abuse in and out of schools. Pray that our children or we do not become an alcoholic. Pray that we as parents and the teacher will continually be stimulated and motivated to teach them.

Pray that all students have a desire to learn and keep learning.

Pray that we be saved to and share God's Love with them. Pray that we as parents will be an inspiration to our children and help them to be all they can be with God. Pray that we as parents, if not saved, become saved and teach our children the benefits of prayers in their life.

When we depend on prayer, we can commit to living out our faith and loving all who are made in God's image. As we cry out to God, He'll help us break down barriers and build bridges of peace with each other. How can you build a bridge of peace between you and others? When have you seen your faithfulness in prayer bear fruit? Heavenly Father please strengthen us to come together with others, fully committed to loving others and living peacefully. The devil is like a germ, creating a contagion more deadly than cancer and aids, only prayer can stop the virus. Anywhere he goes can he infect whoever is around him. Only when people have been injected by the Holy Spirit and daily prayer vitamins, can they survive. The family and church are at high risk. Therefore, it is important to raise standard in prayer. The devil can get in the home and church so quickly, you wonder how he got in. When you look around, there is confusion and conflict all around. Jesus realized this when He told Satan to get behind Him. Luke 4:1-13.

Refresh your thinking by recalling a few people who have raised the standard of prayer.

1. Paul and Silas raised the standard of prayer in a jail house. Acts 16:23-30.
2. Jesus raised the standard of prayer.
3. Our enslaved parents raised the standard of prayer from wash pot, the cotton field, to down the riverside.

Name some of the people you know who have raised the standard of prayer. Prayer should be self-emptying to the point that we can wait quietly, listen carefully and obey immediately. We should learn the prayer of surrender and be able to give up to God, to the point that we can say, "not my will, but your will be done. We must learn the prayer of abandonment, to give in to divine providence, to say to the Father "Into your hands I gave myself." The prayer of release: Life up into His arms your children, your spouse, your family, your friends, your future hopes and dreams. Hold up to your Heavenly father your enemies, anger and all your concerns. When you shall put it all in His hands, turn around and walk away. He will fix everything for you. This is raising the standard of PRAYER.

The purpose here is to raise the standard of Prayer in daily living and in leadership roles. One cannot raise the standard without lifting. One cannot lift without energy and strength to do what need to be done. Prayer keeps us in contact with Jesus, and Jesus gives us the power to carry out His will.

Prayer changes things and people. The primary purpose of prayer is to bring us into such a life of communion with the Father, that the power of the Spirit, we are conformed to the image of the Son.

"Lord Jesus, there is room in my heart for you. I Still Have a Praise In Me!"

I Still Have A Praise In Me

Chapter 6

"Perilous Times"
2Timothy 3:1, "This know also, that is the last days perilous times shall come. People will be lovers of themselves, lovers of money, boastful, proud, abusive, disobedient to their parents, ungrateful, unholy, without love, unforgiving, slanderous, without self-control, brutal, not lovers of the good, treacherous, rash, conceited, lovers of pleasure rather than lovers of God—having a form of godliness but denying its power. Have nothing to do with such people.

Perilous means "difficult", "hard to deal with", or "dangerous". How do we live for Christ in such terrible times? The person who is looking for a soon-coming paradise on earth is destined for disappointment. To expect these perilous times is to become not a pessimist but a realist.

The last days began with the Birth of Christ and will end in Christ's return to the earth to set up His Kingdom. Perilous times would be times of uncertainly. It will be dangerous times. Some believe that we are speaking of the days we now live in. Satanic deception is rampant today and has infected the church and the only weapon that defeats the deceivers is God's inspired Word. Satan is an imitator who produces counterfeit Christians who infiltrate the Church and create divisions. False teaching has come into the Church. People have itching ears. They want a message that sounds good and pleasing to the ear. The Word of God must be told and must be the true Word of God. Some people are constantly looking for something new. They read every how to book they can and never read the Bible. The Bible has the answers to all of life problems. Look there first. The Bible is the Truth. God's people need discernment in these difficult days.

Christ is coming; this we know is certain! In view of this, we must know our task and be faithful to do it.

Apostasy is coming, indeed, is now here! Many professed Christians have no "ear" for the Word of God. They prefer religious entertainment and sermons that will tickle their ears instead of cutting their hearts.

Departure is coming! Paul saw his approaching death as the offering of a sacrifice to God, the ending of a difficult race and the gaining of a glorious crown. This is the victor's crown.

Today in these perilous times, we see war against the family. Our children are being robbed of their innocence. So many of them are being molested, raped and murdered. Many by family members and people they know. These are our babies being taken away from us. So much random violence, so much filthy language and so much sex.

Sex crimes are all over the news. We see today, more and more women who have faced some sort of sexual crisis or period coming forth. For years this has been hidden. I am of the "Me Too Movement". I was raped on my junior/senior prom night on 1970 by my prom date, A.J. This was so long ago. 48 years, so I can't remember all the details, but I know how I felt. I often think of this and told my husband of my experience. I was so hurt and felt so shamed. I never told my parents about this because I was too ashamed and was afraid. Sex was not something we talked about in my family or home. I never told any of my friends or sibling because I was too ashamed. When I returned to school the following week, I felt like everybody was looking at me, pointing fingers and talking. Was it my fault? Did I deserve this? Did I do something? I was all alone. Even to this day, this haunts me. The "Me Too Movement" has made me face up to what happened to me and was able to tell my husband. Even though, I am questioned why I kept silence after so many years, or why I didn't just run or get out of the car, I still felt I had to tell. I was young, naive, inexperienced, afraid and ashamed. When a women or girl says, "NO," she means "NO! For me, seeing so many come forth, has helped me and helped me to accept and know, it was not my fault. I encourage all women and girls to no longer keep silent, but talk and tell somebody. If you can, run and get away. It is not your fault, and you do not deserve to be treated this way. To all those who are coming forth, Thank You so much.

In these perilous times, we see more and more broken homes and divorce. There are so many divorces in our society today, that a child must think who the parents are. Many grandparents are raising their grandchildren, because of divorce, drugs, or worse. Marriage has become obsolete. We see more and more children being born out of wedlock. There are fewer marriage because now many people just live together. The Bible calls this adultery. In these perilous times, we see children, family who put away their parents when they grow old. I Thank God, for my Mother and my Father and giving me the love and strength to be there for them in their last days. We see many who push their parents off on someone else who does not know them. We see more and more mothers abandoning their children. We see women who are destroying their unborn children.

I come from a large family. I have three sisters, Linda (the Late Felix) Dumas, Monna (Timothy) Green, Yolanda Johnson and four brothers, Terry (Denise) Smith, Kemon Smith, Donald (Lisa) Smith and the Late Jessel Smith Jr. Yes, we have our differences, but we do love each other. Sometimes, I feel like I am all alone, an outcast, but I have learned if I call them, they are there. We all have our ways and dislikes, and our private lives. Family are like fudge, sweet with a few nuts mixed in. But if you are like me, you still love them. The love of a family is life's great blessing. Love may have its ups and downs, but love never fails. Life moments make the best memories. The time you spend with family is well spent. We should love each other and each day as a gift. May God make our love awesome and overflow for each other and for everyone else.

In these perilous times, we see so many children being given so many things they did not earn. They have the idea that we owe them this. They have not been taught to work for they want or to earn it. They have not been taught to be obedience and to wait for special occasion. They want it now, and parents are giving it to them and many of them can't afford it. We give it to them because we are afraid of our kids. The child that grows up believing himself to be the center of everything, finds it difficult to put God at the center of his life. They can easily fall into being lovers of their own self. The kids are raising the parents, not the parents raising the kids. In these perilous times, there is so much violence and crime in school; rampant school shooting. So many innocent kids losing their lives and kids who are doing the shooting. Schools used to be the safest place that you could send your kids. Now we have to pray for our kids before going to school and while they are at school. We are living in perilous time.

The media plays a big role, a big responsibility in what is happening in our world today. The media promotes drugs, violence, gambling, adultery, and sex. The music our kids listen to is all about sex, gang violence, shootings, family betrayal, drugs, police shooting, etc. We have so much corruption in our entertainment. Our soap operas are about sex and murder. They are telling our kids it's okay for men to be with men and women with women. Homosexuals live together and called it an alternate lifestyle. God calls it an abominable sin. Everybody fighting for their rights to do wrong!

Talk with and listen to your children. Promote positive behavior and self-responsibility in your child. Be your child's first source of information. Learn how your child develops and know that your child is unique. Cherish your child's individuality. Make time for family activities. Teach your child right from wrong. Take care of yourself.

2 Timothy 3:3, "Without natural affection, trucebreakers, false accusers, incontinent, fierce, despisers of those that are good."

In these perilous times, we see more and more drug use and overdoses. There are drugs on the streets that I and so many cannot name or have heard of. I was in the hospital with a relative when I first heard of "Mojo". The Doctor came in to me and told me that he had overdose on "Mojo", and I asked him what is "Mojo? I was completely innocent and had no idea what he was talking about. He looked at me with a surprised look as if I knew and I had to explain. "Look I am not from the streets; I don't do drugs; I don't smoke; I don't drink, so explain!"

Our kids and even adults see and hear all this, and they are having a hard time, great difficulty evaluating what is good and what is bad. Why is there so much violence and killing? Why are there so many rapes, fights, and robberies? We are in perilous times. We must pray. We must return to God. We as parents have become lacking in our Christian involvement and the things of God. We would rather go to a sporting events, a party, or social gathering, than to Church or prayer meeting. We are more involved in our jobs, our entertainments and other things, than going to Church, Prayer Meeting or Bible Class.

Signs of His Coming...Matthew 24:3, "the disciples came to him privately, saying, tell us, when this will be, and what will be the sign of your coming and the close of the age?"

Does "perilous" describe the condition of the world in which we live? A time where anything goes, right is wrong and wrong is right, mothers against daughters, fathers against sons, unrestraint of every kind imaginable, everyone doing right in their own eyes, fornication and adultery running rampant, disobedient and wayward children, no respect for authority, etc.

The Apostle Paul tells us that the hearts of people in the last days are lovers of themselves, lovers of money, boastful, proud, blasphemers, disobedient to parents, unthankful, unholy, without natural affection, trucebreaker, slanders, unrestrained, fierce, despisers of those who are good, traitors, reckless, conceited, lovers of pleasure more than lovers of God, have a form of godliness, but denying its powers. This is the characteristic that is in our world today.

Today we have war and rumors of wars, Matthew 24:6, "and ye shall hear of wars and rumors of wars: see that ye be not trouble: or all these things must come to pass, but the end is not near."

There will be earthquakes, pestilence and famines in diver's places.

Pestilences is increasing each year. So are AIDS, venereal diseases, STD, anthrax, biological warfare, etc.

Luke 21:11, "And there will be great earthquakes in various places and famine and pestilences; and there will be fearful sights and great signs from heaven."

The video games that our children play are all about sodomy, pornography, sex, blood, and violence. It all kills, kill, kill. There is violence, terrorism, crime, corruption, lying, cheating, and stealing.

We see women ruling and our men effeminate (having feminine qualities typical of a man). They are not leaders in their own home or the Church. 1 Corinthians 6:9, "Or do you know that wrongdoers will not inherit the kingdom of God? Do not be deceived: Neither the sexual immoral nor idolaters nor adulterers nor men who have sex with men."

Children are disobedient to their parents, 2 Timothy 3:2, "for men shall be lovers of their own selves, covetous, boasters, proud, blasphemers, disobedient to parents, unthankful, unholy."

There is an increase in astrology, Satanism, witchcraft and demon activities, 1 Timothy 4:1, "The Spirit clearly says that in later times some will abandon the faith and follow deceiving spirits and things taught by demons."

There is violence, terrorism, crime, corruption, lying, cheating and stealing.

There is false Christ and religion. Matthew 24:24, "For false messiahs and false prophets will appear and perform great signs and wonders to deceive, if possible, even the elect."

People will not endure sound doctrine, 2 Timothy 4:3-4, 'For the time will come when they will not endure sound doctrine; but after their own lusts shall they heap to themselves teachers, having itching ears. And they shall turn away their ears from the truth and shall be turned unto fables."

There will be a falling away and Matthew 24 tells us that during the last days many will turn away from the faith and will betray and hate each other and many false prophets will appear and deceive many people. There will be increase of wickedness, the love of most will grow cold, wars and rumors of wars, but the end is NOT yet.

We are warned in the Scripture about the days ahead and since we are warned, it would be wise for us who claim to belong to Christ to stay ready and don't know Him to get prepared to one day meet Christ. In other words, it is time to get your house in order if you plan to spend eternity with Christ. These are sign of Christ's return. When will He return? No man knows the day or the hour, but God has given us signs throughout the Scripture of what will be happening in the world when Christ makes His second return to gather up His people who belongs to Him. Jesus did not give us the time, but He gave us many signs to look for. Jesus tells us that perilous times will be terrible days ahead of His coming. Things will get worse before they get better.

At Christmas we celebrate the first appearing, which was quiet - the shepherds, the star and the manger. His Second Coming will be with His warriors from heaven to cope with any situation and to defeat the enemies of God until he has subdued the entire world.

The Second Coming of Jesus Christ will be a series of events transpiring over a long period. There are many debates among theologians as to what some of these passages mean, but one thing I know and many others who loves Jesus Christ agree on is that Jesus Christ is coming back.

When He came the first time, He dealt with evil as individual and hereditary. When He comes again, Christ will deal with the practice of evil. He will institute an age of such benevolence that evil cannot reign, and cruelty, oppression and slavery will no longer exist. All this will come to pass as a result of Christ, following His return.

For the true believers of Jesus Christ, the future is assured. Tomorrow belongs to you. We wait for the sound of the trumpet announcing the coming of Jesus Christ. The Christian looks to that tomorrow when the Kingdom of God shall reign.

We have hope for this hour. Matthew 24:44, "Therefore you must be ready; for the Son of Man is coming at an hour you do not expect."

Have you ever had something unexpected happen to you? Surprises can be fun, or they can be disastrous, depending on where we are and what we are doing. To get an unexpected check just in time to pay a financial obligation is a welcome surprise. To get a surprise visit from a friend or loved one you have seen in a while could be a welcome surprise. An unpleasant surprise might be a terrible traffic accident, a death of a loved one, overdrawn bank account, sickness, or divorce. So many things can come by surprise and may not be welcomed.

The return of Christ is going to be a surprise, too. It will be the most glorious and wonderful surprise of all for those who know Him and have committed their lives to Him. For those who are alive, their bodies will be transformed, "in the twinkling of an eye" and they will meet Christ in the air! Imagine what a surprise that will be. You are going about your daily routine when, suddenly and without warning, your body is completely transformed into the likeness of Christ's resurrected body and you "take off" to meet Christ in the air.

For those who do not know Christ, His return will also be a surprise, but a very unpleasant one. For the Judgement will soon follow and those without Christ will spend eternity in hell.

In these last days, perilous times, I advise you to stay connected to God through prayers and The Word of God. Hold fast to what you know and be true to The Word of God. Please do not waiver in your faith, but believe what God has written in The Bible, in spite of what you hear. Follow Godly leaders that you know are living their lives according to the Word of God. Be not conformed by this world and its temporary pleasure but be ye transformed by the renewing of your mind with the Word of God. Be watchful and alert. Put on the whole armor of God, daily girding yourself with the truth of the Gospel, for an hour we expect not, the Son of Man shall come.

Everything we need to know about going to Heaven can be found in the Bible. God has not kept His Word from us but has revealed it to ALL who trust Him and believe.   The Word of God is sufficient in and of itself.

The Bible is the Christian's sword by which we fight the battle of life. But a sword does no good if it is left of the tables or on the shelf. You have to take it out and use it. Read, study, meditate day and night.

Please stay alert because the enemy is lurking, seeking whom he may devour. Please don't let it be you.

We should use every opportunity we have to tell others of our glorious Savior who wants all to meet Him in the air and to live with Him forever.

Perilous times would be times of great uncertainty and dangerous times. I am sure that you would agree that we are in perilous times, the last days.

The God who promises to never leave or forsake us (Hebrew 13:5) is the One we trust with our lives every day. Although we live in a dangerous world, our God gives us peace and assurance-both now and forever. He is our safe place. The world around me can feel threatening, overwhelming and dangerous. But God give me peace, strength and help. I give God thanks for being my hiding place.

Help is coming! Jesus will never leave you or forsake you. "I Still Have A Praise In Me."

Chapter 7

Stress of a Black Woman
Philippians 4:6-7, "Do not be anxious about anything, but in everything by prayer and supplication with thanksgiving let your request be known to God. And the peace of God which surpasses all understanding will guard your hearts and your minds in Christ Jesus."

Stress can impact a person in different ways, not just mentally, but also physically. It can have a significant negative effect on your body and mind which trickles down into relationship, work, as well as overall health and well-being.

While a little stress can be healthy, it can also push you to put in more effort in both your personal and professional life without any severe problem. Being stressed out all the time, or on a regular basis is detrimental your health.

Some of the symptom that I have experience of stress is lack of sleep, headache, bizarre and recurring dreams, jaw and tooth pain, grinding teeth while asleep, hair loss, weight loss and gain, stomachache and intestinal problems, ulcer, muscle tension, joint pain, poor diet, high blood pressure, lack of self-worth and depression, loss of sex drive, hopelessness and apathy, can't concentrate, just don't care, not liking self, withdrawn from people, fantasy of ways to escape, and suicide. Stress can impact a person in many different ways, not just mentally but physically.

Psalm 46:1-3, "God is our refuge and strength, a very present help in trouble. Therefore, will we fear, though the earth be removed, and though the mountains be carried into the midst of the sea. Though the waters thereof roar and be trouble, through the mountains shake with the swelling thereof. Selah."

The key words in these verses are "God is our refuges and strength." He is always ready to help in times of trouble and stress, so we will not be afraid.

I think God is calling us, the Black Woman during these times. Remember God is our refuge. He is our strength, so we should have no fear, no matter what comes our way. God is reminding us to be still and know that He is God, know that God is in control, and know that God will provide. He will make a way. In God we can find our true security, no matter what happens in our lives.

It is easy to doubt God in times of trouble. It is easy to doubt God when we are stressed out over things that happen to us. It is easy to doubt God when the people that are supposed to love us are causing us stress and so much pain. We have to remember, God is the one we should turn to because He is the one who will bring us through. God will give us WORDS for whatever season it is.

I am stressed, but I am not going to let it get the best of me.

I am stressed, but I know how to pray.

I am stressed. I am human, but God is in control.

God knows all, sees all and He is in control of it all. I serve an awesome God. Satan is really trying to discourage me. Troubled marriage, troubled children, trouble with finance, trouble with sickness, and loss of love ones. No peace or rest.

When life gets messy, it's natural for us as black women to get stressed or angry or bitter, especially when life takes a turn we didn't expect, like a broken marriage, broken engagement, loss of a spouse, diagnosis of cancer or loss of a job. The unexpected mess has happened in my life many times. I have learned that most of the time that troubles come, God wants to sharpen us, mold us and transform us into something greater. He wants us to see a side of

Himself that we haven't yet seen. He wants others to see the amazing things that He can do in our lives when we trust Him with the mess. So, we might as respond the way He desires so we get out of the mess, don't you think?

There are lots of reasons that I can come up with not to trust God when life takes a turn for the worse. The alternative to trust is stress. Stress kills, literally and can cause permanent damage. So, I will save my health, pass the test and please God by trusting Him in the middle of the mess.

I will trust God with my tears and not stress when I am in the middle of the mess because God is more compassionate. Psalm 56:8 tells me that God not only sees my tears, he collects them. That means my hurt is more precious to Him then I can imagine.

My situation didn't take God by surprise. Just because it caught me off guard, doesn't mean that God was clueless. Psalm 139 tells me that God is familiar with all my ways, where I've been and what I am doing and where I am going. Before there is a word on my tongue, God already knows it.

God is much more capable of managing my life than I am. I often believe that I have the best solutions to my problems. There are times I've found myself suggesting to God what He ought to do in certain situation, but Isaiah 55:8-9 assure me that His ways are higher than my ways, meaning His method and His timing in how He chooses to do things are so much better than mine. He is God, and I am not and that just might be what He's trying to show me in the struggling I am trying to fix. I just have to give it to Him, and He will handle it.

God can, at any time, clear up the mess, so I have to wait on His timing and learn all He wants me to learn in the moment. Roman 8:28 assures me that "God causes all things to work together for good to those who love God to His purpose." The next verse tells me that "God works things for good in our lives, for those whom he foreknew, he also predestined to become conformed to the image of his Son" …There it is. God wants me to become more like His Son through my struggles. So, I will be teachable. I will be open to what He wants me to learn, and I will be moldable. My heart might be the reason God has not yet fixed the situation.

God is incapable of misunderstanding, mismanagement or mistakes. Deuteronomy 32:4 says, "His works are perfect and all His are just." That means God doesn't get it wrong. I, on the other hand, am capable of making an even greater mess of things. I have to quit my meddling and let God work His miracle.

God already has the problem solved. I am always looking for a certain resolution before I consider the problem fixed. God looks to the details of my intentions and my very heart. It possible the problem still exists because He is working on something inside me right now and then He'll take care of the exterior situation.

A messy situation is one of the primary ways God awakens my need for Him, shapes my character and draws me closer to Him. Life consist of messes of problems. They are not because I did something wrong. Sometimes it happens. Often, He allows it because He wants to draw me into a deeper dependence on Him and to show me a new side of Himself. Those things that make my messes meaningful—draws me closer to my Savior. James 1:2-3, "consider it all joy" when we encounter various trials, knowing the testing of our faith produces endurance." And let endurance have its perfect result, so that I may be perfect and complete, lacking nothing (Verse 4).

God can be trusted. He wants me to know that. I will continue to lean on Him during my trials and messes.

A woman will never get the respect she deserves until she forces her man or spouse to understand that she is a woman with options who can be bad all by herself. It is easy to be negative, but it takes a person with courage and strength to face all challenge of life and stay positive. Sometimes you have to laugh through the tears, smile through the pain so that you can live through the sorrow. Never judge a person by what the other person tells you.

But it's all good. I will give it to God. Let Go and Let God. God is my refuge and my strength. God is always ready to help in times of trouble.

Psalm 27:1, "The Lord is my light and my salvation, whom shall I fear? The Lord is the strength of my life; I shall not be afraid." The first step to stress is to admit and give it to God. God may send a load, but He will not send a neglect. Depression and stress are old as human being. The Bible has many who struggle with depression and stress.

Elijah in his depression and fatigue, ask God for his life to be taken away.

Jonah was deeply despondent after God did not destroy Nineveh.

Jeremiah regretted the day he was born.

Job's wife advised him to curse God and die in the midst of his suffering and pain.

Depression and stress have no respect of person. People of both genders, rich or poor, and nationally get depressed and stressed.

There are times in my life that I feel so low and alone. I just want to end it all. I just want to be left alone. There are times that I am in Church that I am so down, that I just can't wait for the service to end, just want to run to the door and don't want to speak to anyone. I feel like everyone is against me, looking at me and taking about me.

Where is God when this happens? Where is your faith? Where is your victorious Christian life? Where is the peace that support all understanding? Where is the faith that you have told others about and experience? How am I supposed to deal with this? Do I act like I am okay when I am drowning, sad, and alone? What am I to do? Do I go out and try something new? Do I eat or just turn on the TV? Do I get in bed and put the covers over my head? Do I have an affair? Do I pretend it doesn't exist? What do I do?

Depression and stress are real. They have physical issues, spiritually issues and psychological issues. What Do I do?

God understand my stress and my depression. Here is what I do. I will ask God for help. I will ask Him to hear me. I will seek Him for help. God understand me, and He will help me. Please get some help, tell somebody that you can trust what you are going through. You are not alone.

Depression and stress are not a sin. It is message that we need help and are in trouble.

Woman that are led by God are dangerous. They can achieve all things with or without the help or guidance of a man. Every man has the power to be the best boyfriend, husband, and person he can be to a woman. It all depends on when he is ready to grow up. Black women are strong, intelligent and are beautiful. They are mothers who love her children. She loves her children in ways that they will never understand. All her children are special.

Black women know how to admit when they are wrong and are not afraid to apologize. An apology does not mean you are wrong or the other is right, it just means you value your relationship and your marriage more than your ego. We don't need a perfect relationship. We need somebody who will be there for us no matter what.

Black Woman, every day is a blessing. Don't take the people God has put in your life for granted. God's plan is the best plan and

God has a reason for everything.   Don't stress out on things that are out of your control. We as Black Women don't ask for much but deserves everything.

It is better to be alone at peace than to be surrounded by drama-filled friends.   People need to learn that their actions do affect other people. So be careful what you say and do. It is not always about you.

And Black Women, just let me say this, if you got a man lying around you and you are broke and stressed out, ask yourself, what purpose is that man?

God I just want to take a moment not to ask for anything from you, but to just say Thank You! You always hear and answer prayers. You may not always answer when I want you to, but you will when the time is right. I have to learn to be patient.

You feel inadequate because you seem to lack something, a university degree, a loving spouse, a child, a job, or a house. Well, just keep living for Him faithfully and waiting patiently for Him and His plan, just as Elizabeth did. No matter our circumstances, God is working in and through us. He knows our heart and He hears our prayers. God is faithful and good. Just keep trusting in Him even when you experience heartache. Keep living for Him faithfully and waiting patiently for His plan.

At some point, we as Black Women, we all find ourselves in situations that can causes us despair. It could be a bad medical report, a sudden job loss, or a shattered family. When life knocks us down, we can still look up, for God is still on the throne! He holds our days in His hands, and He hold us close to His heart. Continue to pray that God fills you with hope and gives you a reminder that things will turn outright in His way and in His time. The world hopes for the best, but the Lord offers the best hope.

O Lord my God let me see me through your eyes! John 14:18, "I will never you comfortless.'

Psalm 11:117, "The Lord is on my side.'

With the above Scripture and this poem, you can find encouragement.

"Don't Quit'
When things go wrong, as they sometimes will,
When the road you're trudging seem all up hill,
When the fund is low, and the debts are high
and you want to smile, but you have to sigh.
When the care is pressuring you down a bit,
Rest if you must, but don't quit.

Life is strange with its twists and turns.
 As everyone of us sometimes learns.
And many a failure turns about.
When he might have won had he stuck it out
Don't give up though the pace seems slow.
You may succeed with another blow.

Success is failure turned inside out.
The silver tint of the clouds of doubt.
And you can never tell how close you are.
It may be near when it seems so far.
 So stick to the fight when you're hardest hit.
It's when thing seem worst
That you must not quit.

In Jesus Name, I pray, Amen.

This will be my next book, "Black Women, "The Face Behind The Mask".

Through it all, "I Still Have A Praise In Me.

Chapter 8

The Character of Love In The Home by Rev. Vernon Alexander
Sr.
1Timothy 3:1-5, "Here is a trustworthy saying: Whosoever aspire
to be an overseer desire a noble task."

Now the overseer is to be above reproach, faithful to his wife,
temperate, self-controlled, respectable, hospitable, able to teach,
not given to drunkenness, not violent but gentle, not quarrelsome,
not a lover of money. He must manage his own family well and
see that his children obey him, and he must do so in a manner
worthy of full respect. If anyone does not know how to manage
his own family, how can he take care of God's church?

If anyone wants to provide leadership in the church good! But
there are preconditions.

When dealing with character, let us first begin with the nature of
God—Love. God is Love and therefore the character of Christ is
the character of Love. For the minister, this love-walk originates
in relationship with God and translate into domestic realm.

As the old adage goes, charity begins at home. Hence, the
character of Christ must be reflected in a minister's loving
commitment to his or her spouse, this is important because the
natural relationship between the husband and wife visually depicts
the spiritual relationship between Christ and His Church.
Therefore, a husband that does not love his wife or a wife that does
not submit to her husband has no business preaching, they are not
qualified! The character of love is not manifest in the home.

As ministers, our children must be obedient to us. Though Paul does not reference age, his inference clearly indicates minor children. Paul says in 1 Timothy 3:4, "One that rules well his own house having his children in subjection with all gravity."

These criteria encompass the domestic realm; husband, wife, children. Paul then moved from domestic realm to the character of love in the church.
Ephesians 5:25-28, "Husbands, go all out in your love for your wives, exactly as Christ did for the church—a love marked by giving, not getting." Christ's love makes the church whole. His words evoke her beauty. Everything he does and says is designed to bring the best out in her, dressing her in dazzling white silk, radiant with holiness. And this is how husbands ought to love their wives. They're really doing themselves a favor since they're already "one" in marriage."

This passage is picturesque of Christ's love for the Church. If we as ministers say we love Christ, we must also love what He loves; and Christ loves the Church. When our love for the Church is found wanting—like an avid swimmer that does not like water— we are essentially a walking contradiction. However, as we grow in our love for Christ, our love for His Church comes naturally.

This love will manifest in several ways. First, it is reflected in our adherence to regular church attendance. Since God has called us to ministry, we must be connected to a local church. In so doing, not only do we receive teaching and instruction, but also, we become biblical examples of Hebrews 10:25, "Not forsaking the assembling of ourselves together, as the manner of some is; but exhorting one another: and so much the more, as ye see the day approaching."

A second attribute of our love for the Lord's Church is serving in a local assembly with our time, talent, gifts, possessions and money.

God loves you, The Believers. John 3:16, "For God so loves the world that he gave his one and only Son, that whoever believes in him shall not perish but have eternal life."

Roman 5:8, "But God demonstrated his own love for us in this: While we were still sinners, Christ died for us."

Listen to Jesus. John 10:17, "The reason my Father loves me is that I lay down my life—only to take it up again. No man takes it from me, but I lay it down of my own accord. I have authority to lay it down and authority to take it up again. This commandment I received from my Father."

John 15:13, "Greater love has no one than this: to lay down one's life for one's friends."

Jesus died on the Cross because He loves us. He rose again. He is coming back because He loves us.

There were three man on the cross. Jesus was between the two. One man's sin was in him and on him and the other man's sin, was in him but not on him, because He said Lord when you enter into your Kingdom remember me. Jesus took this man's sin on Him. Jesus hung on the Cross, but He had no sin in Him, but He had sin on Him. He took on our sin, so that we could have eternal life. He is now sitting at the right Hand of God making intersession for us and one day, He will return for us, the believers and we will be with Him forever. Are you ready for His return?

We may grow older and the world around us may change, but God's Love doesn't change. He can always be trusted to take care of those who turn to Him. We should be thankful to God for His Love that never changed. Ask God to help us to love Him by serving Him faithfully today and every day.

Ten Commandments for the Home, Psalm 28:9, "Save thy people and bless thine inheritance."

What shall it profit men or women if they gain the whole world, but lose their own families? With a 50 percent divorce rate and more two wage-earner households, the home as we have known it in the past, indeed, as God established it, is truly an endangered species. Marriage and the family were not quaint ideas cooked up by society. The family was ordained of God before He established any other institution, even before He established the Church.

I want to suggest ten commandments for a solid, happy, God-honoring home:
1.   Establish God's chain of command. The Bible teaches that for the Christian, Jesus Christ is to head the home, with the wife under authority of a Christlike husband and the children responsible to their parents,
2.   Obey the commandment that you love one another,
3.   Show acceptance and appreciation for each family member.
4.   It is important to have training and discipline in the home and not just for the family dog!
5.   Family members should respect God's authority over them, and the authority God has delegated down the chain of command.
6.   Enjoy one another and take time to enjoy family life together. Quality time is no substitute for quantity time. Quantity time is quality time.
7.   Do not commit adultery. Adultery destroys a marriage and is a sin against God and against your mate.
8.   Everyone in a family should work together for the mutual benefit of the family. No child should be without chores or without the knowledge that works brings fulfillment.
9.   Pray together and read the Bible together. Nothing strengthens a marriage and family more. Nothing is a better defense against Satan.
10.   Every family member should be concerned about whether every other member of the family is saved. This extends from the immediate family to grandparents, uncles, aunts, cousins and in-laws.

No one is truly a success in God's eyes if his family is a mess. I Still Have a Praise In Me!"

Loving God, thank You for Your Love. Help us to trust in and follow Your light and love even when the way gets dark.

I Still Have A Praise In Me

Chapter 9

"The Best Is Yet To Come"
Sermon by Rev. Joseph Comminie
1 Corinthians 2: 7-9, "No, we declare God's wisdom, a mystery that has been hidden and that God destined for our glory before time began, none of the rulers of this age understood it, for if they had, they would have not crucified the Lord of glory. However, as it is written: "What no eye has seen, what no ear has heard, and what no human mind has conceived: the things God has prepared for those who love him."

You must have a spiritual vision and a spiritual mind to understand what Paul is saying and what the preacher is unveiling. The Apostle Paul wrote these words under the guidance of the Holy Spirit. He was inspired by the Spirit of God to write. Eyes hath not seen, nor ears heard, neither have entered into the heart of man the things which God hath prepared for them that love Him. Paul had planted a Church in a city, but the city had gotten into the Church, The Church at Corinth had been victimized by Satan.

As believers in the Blessed Savior, we are constantly being victimized by Satan. Young children, young adult, whatever you want to say, are being victimized by Satan. All over the land, in our Churches, in our school, in our homes.

It is Satan's plan to throw you, to throw us off the divine course. These Christians at Corinth had started off good. They were very enthused about being born again. But they were thrown off course, for one thing, they forgot the calling that they had in the Blessed Christ. Just as some of us have.

These believers started following human leaders and developed a fan club mentality. They started depending more on human wisdom and philosophies, than on the wisdom of God. They forgot that Christ Jesus died and now lives to bless His sheep. The Believers' faith should not stand in the wisdom of man, but in the power of God. Man's wisdom says get all you can get here. Eat drink and be merry. But I am saying to you, "The Best Is Yet to Come".

Many Christians, young and old are being distracted by the Devil's schemes. We want to have it our way. We want to do things our way. We are more concerned with satisfying our physical desires and not concern with spiritual and eternal things. We sometimes live for the temporary and immediate, not the eternal. That is what happened to the believers at Corinth. They lost their motivation for Christ.

You see, the Blessed Christ is the only one that can keep our Spiritual interest high. We must keep our eyes on Christ Jesus because He alone is the Captain of our Salvation.

There is a better place than this mean cruel world, Paul said in 2 Corinthians 5:1, 'we have a building of God, a house not made with hands, eternal in the Heaven "Jesus said in John 14:2, "In my Father's House are many mansions".

How we live today will help determine our place in the future Kingdom of Christ. In this present age, we see man fallen in Adam. But by faith, we see Christ and His victory. We see the Church still marching. Because Christ is glorified, all these that have been wash in the blood of the Lamb shall be glorified one day. Because "The Best Is Yet To Come." There is a day coming when the dead in Christ shall get up, and we which are alive and remain shall be caught up. Let me remind you that your Salvation is calling. We were chosen by the Father who give us the new birth. We are set apart by the Holy Ghost who gave the Word and enable us to declare it. We have been purchased by the blood of

70

God's Son who died and rose and is coming back to give back their inheritance. We have become heirs with Christ, and we may think we have it good here, but "The Best Is Yet To Come". Saints of God, you must never lose your motivation for Christ. You must never lose you love for Christ. We must set our sights on eternal things.

The Blessed Savior said in Matthew 6:20, "Lay not up for yourselves treasure upon earth where moth and rust doth corrupt and where thieves break through and steal. But lay up for yourselves treasure in Heaven where neither moth nor rust doth corrupt. For where your treasure is there will your heart be also."

The Believers at Corinth had lost their first Love. They weren't motivated anymore, and they became worldly. The Devil's influence made things around them seem attractive. It is no different today. We have more Christians adapting to the way of the world. We talk like them. We live like them. We curse like them. 2 Corinthians 6:14 says, "For what fellowship hath righteousness with unrighteousness?" Or what fellowship can lights have with darkness?

2 Corinthians 6:15-16, "What harmony has Christ with Belial, or what has a believer in common with unbelievers?' And what agreement hath the temple of God with idols; for ye are the temple of the living God,"

The Church has to remember that we have a living hope even though we are surrounded by corruption and every conceivable sin. Even though you feel pressure to adapt to the environment, we must hold on to God's unchanging hands. That is why our Pastors and Leaders must keep sounding the trumpet because the people of God has fallen in love with the world.

James said, in James 4:4, "whosoever therefore will be a friend of the world is the enemy of God." And 1 John 2:15 says, "Love not the world, neither the things that are in the world, if any man love the world, the love of the Father is not in him."

The Holy God has something in store for His people. "The Best Is Yet to Come". We must keep fighting sin with faith. Faith is God will keep us on the right track. 1 Peter 2:9, "You are a chosen generation, a royal priesthood, a holy nation, a peculiar people. You should shew forth the praises of Him who hath called you out of darkness into His marvelous light."

How can we expect to keep our children on track when we are so far off track? We have to know who we are. I wonder sometimes about some Christians. I have to wonder if they really believe that "The Best Is Yet To Come". We must be about our Father's business. Obedience is better than sacrifice. We must walk worthy of the vocation wherewith we are called.

Paul in his admonition to the Church at Ephesus said in Ephesians 6:1, "Children obey your parents in the Lord, for this is right. Honor thy Father and Mother which is the first commandment with promise that it may be well with thee and thou mayest live long on the earth." Not only will you live a long and prosperous life here, but you will have an eternal home with the Blessed Savior. You must realize "The Best Is Yet to Come".

1 Peter 5:4, "And when the chief Shepherd shall appear, ye shall receive a crown of glory that fadeth not away.

1 Peter 1:4, 'you have an inheritance, incorruptible and undefiled, reserved in Heaven for you."

Heaven is so wonderful. The only way John could describe it is to tell us what will be there. John wrote no more sin, no pain, no death, nor sorrow or crying! That is why I know in my heart that "The Best Is Yet To Come."

Children and Saints of God, we are not philosophers living on
man's explanations. We are pilgrims living of God. And God
never fails, and God never lies. Jesus said in, Matthew 24:35,
'Heaven and earth shall pass away, but my Words shall not pass
away."

For all those who believe in the Blessed Christ, the future means
all things new. Human history begins with a garden and will end
with a city like a garden. John said in, Revelation 21:1-2, "I saw a
new heaven and a new earth" for the first heaven and the first earth
had passed away and there was no longer any sea. I saw the Holy
City, the new Jerusalem coming down out of heaven from God,
prepared as a bride beautifully dressed for her husband."

I am going home one day. When things around us look dark,
remind yourself that God will one day fill the earth with His
Glory. The Apostle Paul cried out Thanks be to God who has
given us the victory. To live victoriously, we must realize that
Jesus is the Good Shepherd. If the Lord is your Shepherd, you can
say, I shall not want because the Good Shepherd feeds me, and He
leads me when I wander. He seeks us and restores us as He did
David, Jonah and Peter, when we need to know which way to go.
The Good Shepherd shows us the right path and then goes before
us to prepare the way. If life is difficult Saints, keep trusting the
Good Shepherd. He told us in John 16:33, "In the world you shall
have tribulations: be of good cheer; I have overcome the world."

Righteous living children is not popular today. But one day, it will
be rewarded because "The Best Is Yet to Come." The joyful
anticipation of Christ's return is great motivation for Holy Living
and the Church to be on guard. It is easy to lose what you have
gained by making friends with the wrong person, but I know a
friend that will stick closer than a brother. I know a friend you can
tell all your troubles too. I am talking about Jesus. The song
writer says, "What a friend we have in Jesus." He is a sympathetic
High Priest who can meet our every need. He can sympathize
what you are going through. We must be steadfast, because "The

73

Best is Yet To Come." We must be unmovable, because "The Best Is Yet to Come." Serving God will pay off. The Apostle Paul realized that.

I remember Paul saying in 2 Timothy 4:7-8, "I have fought a good fight. I have finished my course. I have kept the faith. Henceforth there is laid up for me a crown of righteousness, which the Lord, righteousness judge, shall give me that day; and not to me only, but unto all them also that love his appearing." Paul knew that "The Best Is Yet to Come."

We must keep walking by faith and not by sight, because "The Best Is Yet to Come." We must keep running this race with patience, because "The Best Is Yet to Come." We must keep carrying the blood stain banner till we depart because "The Best is Yet to Come." We must endure hardness as good soldiers of Jesus Christ because "The Best Is Yet to Come." We must keep walking as Ambassador of Christ bringing the message of reconciliation. Some may be going through a hard trial, but remember God promise in Deuteronomy 31:6, "I will never leave you nor forsake you. I will be with you always."

In a changing world our God is unchanging. He can pick you up, turn you around, place your feet on solid ground. 2 Corinthians 5:1, "We Know that if our earthly house of this tabernacle were dissolve, we have a building of God. A house not made with hands, eternal in the Heavens".

We have eternal security. Romans 8:31, "If God be for us, who can be against us?"

Romans 8:38-39, "For I am persuaded, that neither death, nor life, nor angels, nor principalities, nor power, nor things present, nor things to come. Neither height nor depth, nor any other creature, shall be able to separate us from the love of God, which is in Christ Jesus Our Lord."

We are not frustrated by the suffering we experience or see in our world because we have hope. When Jesus returns, we will enter into glorious liberty! The Spirit is the beginning of the harvest and assure us that the best is yet to come.

Let us run with patience this race that is set before us. Hebrew 12:2, "Looking to Jesus, the author and finisher of our faith: who for the joy that was set before him endured the cross, despising the shame, and is set down at the right hand of the throne of God."

Jesus paid it all, all to Him I owe. Sin had left the crimson stain, but Jesus washed me white as snow. The song writer says, "There is a fountain filled with blood drawn from Emmanuel's veins. Sinners plunge beneath that flood lose all their guilty stain. That Blood has not lost its power." It's has power to sustain you till the Blessed Jesus comes again. "The Best Is Yet to Come" and I Still Have a Praise In Me!

I Still Have A Praise In Me

Chapter 10:

God to Return
Titus 2:13, "Awaiting our blessed hope, the appearing of the glory
of our God and savior Jesus Christ."

The promised coming of the Lord has been the great hope of true
believers down through the centuries. The great creeds of the
church teach that Christ is coming back. He shall come again with
glory to judge both the living and the dead. The future belongs to
God.

We are troubled by the events and things we read every day in the
newspaper. We are disturbed by what we see on our television
screens, and we are troubled by what we see in our communities.
We are even disturbed and stressed by the problems of our
everyday family life. There are problems we have never been able
to solve. The first is human iniquity. The problem of human
iniquity is lying, hate, lust and greed. When Christ comes back,
He's going to solve that problem.

The next problem is human suffering. We may live in the best
cities, have the best homes, and the best money can buy. Yet we
suffer from a broken heart, loneliness, boredom, physical or mental
suffering. Christ at His return will take away suffering. He says
He will wipe away all tears. There will be no more backaches or
headaches, cancer and heart disease will be eliminated, mental
illness will be no more. All the disease of mankind will be cured
when Christ comes back.

The greatest unsolved problem of all is the crisis of death, which
each of us have to face. It is appointed unto men once to die," says
the Bible. But when Christ returns for His Church, those redeemed

ones who are alive will not die but will be caught up to meet Him in the air. For them, death will be ended.

When Christ comes, peace will come. Our greatest scholars are seeking a way for peace, but they are attempting to do it without the Prince of Peace. Man cannot bring enduring peace. Enduring peace will be brought only when the Prince of Peace comes and sets up His great and mighty kingdom.

As the Christians with the Bible in our hand survey the world scene, we are aware that we do not worship an absentee God. We are aware that God is in the shadows of history and that he has a plan. The Christian is not to be disturbed by the chaos, violence, strife, bloodshed and threat of war that fill our daily news. We know that these things are the consequences of man's sin and greed. If anything else were happening, we would doubt the Bible. Every day we see a thousand evidences of the fulfillment of biblical prophecy. Every day as I read the newspaper I say; "The Bible Is True."

No matter how foreboding the future, the Christian knows the end of the story of history, we are heading toward a glorious climax. "The Best Is Yet To Be."

The Bible indicates that the future is in God's hands. If it were in our hands, we would make a mess of it. The future is not in the devil's hands, for then he would lead us to destruction. The future is not at the mercy of any historical determinism leading us blindly forward, for then life would be without meaning. But the future is in the hands of the One who is preparing something better than eye hath seen, or ear heard, or entered into the heart of man to conceive.

The psalmist said; "The Lord is my light and my salvation, whom shall I fear? The Lord is the strength of my life; whom shall I be afraid?" Psalm 27:1. What make us afraid? Darkness? But the Lord is our light. Danger? He is our salvation. Deficiency? He is our strength. Then why be afraid? See what He does for you and me.

God saves us. Because he was not a priest, David could not actually go into the tabernacle, but he could still rest in the Lord and trust Him as his refuge. In Him is perfect safety.

God smiles on us. We must go beyond merely seeking God's help. Seek His face (Number 6:22-27). The smile of God is all we need to overcome the scowls of men.

God shows us the way. Satan wants to trap us, but the Lord will show us the safe way. Believe His promise and walk by faith. His goodness will be with us.

God strengthens us. We need strength for the battle and strength for the journey and God abundantly provides. Be sure to take time to wait on the Lord. If you run ahead of Him or lag behind, you will be a target for the enemy.

James 5:8, "Be ye also patient; stablish your hearts: for the coming of the Lord drawth nigh."

In these last days, before the coming of the Lord, what does God want in our lives? He wants Priorities. To live only to get wealth is to rob yourself of true riches, it is to worry instead of worship. God knows we have need and He will meet them if we practice Matthew 6:33, "But seek first his kingdom and his righteousness and all these things will be given to you as well."

God wants Patience. If we sow the right seed, we will eventually reap a harvest of blessing, so be patient. If others have exploited you, be patient, The Judge is at the door. If you are going through trials, be patient. God is still on the throne.

God wants Prayer. Many kinds of prayer are named. Prayer for the sick, prayer for forgiveness, prayer for the nation, even prayer for the weather. There is no need that prayer cannot meet and no problem that prayer cannot solve.

God wants Personal Concern. Can we detect when a fellow believer starts to stray? Are we truly concern? Will we try to help? Will we wait too long?

Jesus Christ is absolute truth. Matthew 24 and 25 are entirely given over to statements about His coming. Matthew 24:27, "For as lighting that comes from the east is visible even in the west, so will be coming the Son of Man." The Bible again says in Matthew 25:31-32, "When the Son of man come in his glory and all the holy angels with him, then shall he sit upon the throne of his glory: and before him shall be gathered all nations...." This prophecy has yet to be fulfilled, but He said it and I believe it will be.

Jesus didn't lie to us. He said, "I go to prepare a place for you, and if I go and prepare a place for you, I will come again, and receive you unto myself; that where I am, there ye may be also" John 14:2-3. He is coming back in person. The Lord Jesus is coming back Himself! That's how much He loves us. The plan of Salvation is not only to satisfy us in this world and give us a new life here, but He has a great plan for the future. For eternity!

The Bible says we are going to reign with Him. We're joint heirs with the Lord Jesus Christ and we're going to spend eternity with Him! What is He doing now? He's preparing a home for us! It's been nearly two thousand years. What a home it must be! Eyes cannot see, nor ears hear, not hath entered the heart of man, what God has prepared for those who love Him! In Revelation John wrote, ...The Lord God giveth them light and they shall reign forever...Behold, I come quickly!" Even so, come lord Jesus!

We may appear to be a Christian to the world. We may even profess to being a Christian. My question is, if you were on trial for being a Christian, could you be convicted by the evidence in your life? Would God declare you to be a Christian, by the condition of your heart, or would He say get away from me. I never knew you. Matthew 7:33.

I will examine self. Is my life what it ought to be? Let God test my mind and heart. In my walking, standing and sitting, am I keeping myself clean? Sometime God allows the enemy to attack me just to get me to take time to take a personal inventory. Focus on the Lord. If I look at others, I will be upset and if I look too long, I may get discouraged, so I will focus my attention on the Lord. Match my defects with His perfections and claim what I need from Him.

We look in the mirror to examine ourselves to see if anything needs correction-hair combed, face washed, shirt properly buttoned. Like a mirror, the Bible helps us to examine our character, attitude, thoughts and behavior (James 1:23-24). This enables us to align our lives according to the principles of what God has revealed. We will "keep a tight rein" on our tongues (v. 27). We will pay heed to God's Holy Spirit within us and keep ourselves "from being polluted by the world" (v. 27).

As we look into the mirror of the Scripture, we can "humbly accept the word planted in us" (v. 21). Heavenly Father, "open my eyes that I may see wonderful things in your law" (Psalm 119:18). Help me to order my life according to what You show me in Scripture. As a mirror reflects our image, the Bible reveals our inner being.

Keep serving the Lord. The enemy wants nothing better than to upset me and get me on a detour. I will continue to walk with the Lord and serve Him, come what may. Bless the Lord and don't complain. God will vindicate me in His time and in His own way.

Life is a wonderful gift from the Lord. I honor Him when I take pleasure both in His daily blessings and in meaningful service. God, thank you for this life You've given me. Help me to live for you, enjoying your blessing and fulfilling Your purposes.

Enjoy God's blessing and be a blessing to others.

Love for the Master. As a Christian servant, we love Jesus so much that we give Him our lives. Because we love Him, we serve Him. What the world needs today is not more educators, doctors or lawyer, but people who are willing to surrender to being Christian servants. The mark of a true servant is characterized by a joyful attitude and conduct. A person who is happy, excited and on fire for God is being a servant. This person delights in serving God. He finds personal satisfaction is serving. He serves because it brings pleasure.

The mark of a servant is faithfulness in little matters and big matters. He does not give in or up. A real servant is dependable. He gives his or her best and serves until death. The mark of a servant is one who is characterized by a low profile. The mark of a servant is one who will not draw attention to self and demand his or her will. The mark of a true servant is one who accepts a position, task or role that allows him or her to meet the need of others.

The Mark of a Servant - Part of the difficulty in being a servant comes from the fact that someone else get the credit we feel we deserve. We want to be recognized and be considered important. We need to remember the sign that read, "There is no limit to what a man can do if he doesn't care who gets the credit."
"I Still Have A Praise In Me"

Psalm 27, "The Lord is my light and my salvation-whom shall I fear? The Lord is the stronghold of my life - of whom shall I be afraid? When the wicked advance against me to devour me, it is my enemies and my foes who will stumble and fall. Though an army besiege me, my heart will not fear.

Though war breaks out against me, even then will I be confident.

One thing I ask from the Lord all the days of my life, to gaze on the beauty of the Lord and to seek him in his temple. For in the day of trouble he will keep me safe in his dwelling. He will hide me in the shelter of his sacred tent and set me high upon a rock.

Then my head will be exalted above the enemies who surround me. At his scared tent I will sacrifice with shouts of joy. I will sing and make music to the Lord.

Hear my voice when I call, Lord; be merciful to me and answer me. My heart says of you, "Seek his face!" Your face, Lord I will seek. Do not hide your face from me, do not turn your servant away in anger; you have been my helper. Do not reject me or forsake me, God my Savior.

Though my father and mother forsake me, the Lord will receive me. Teach me your way, Lord. Lead me in a straight path because of my oppressors. Do not turn me over to the desire of my foes, for false witness rise up against me, spouting malicious accusations.

I remain confident of this: I will see the goodness of the Lord in the land of the living, wait on the Lord; be strong and take heart and wait on the Lord.
. . . .
Pray when surrounded by trouble, problems or wickedness. God is our only real source of safety. Prayer is our best help when trials comes our way because it keeps us in communion with God.

Gail Marie Comminie

I Still Have A Praise In Me

Gail Marie Comminie

I Still Have A Praise In Me

CPSIA information can be obtained
at www.ICGtesting.com
Printed in the USA
BVHW071346120820
586216BV00007B/244

9 781951 497286